From Hubble to Hubble Astronomers and Outer Space

Connie Jankowski

Earth and Space Science Readers:
From Hubble to Hubble: Astronomers and Outer Space

Publishing Credits

Editorial Director
Dona Herweck Rice

Creative Director
Lee Aucoin

Associate Editor
Joshua BishopRoby

Illustration Manager
Timothy J. Bradley

Editor-in-Chief
Sharon Coan, M.S.Ed.

Publisher
Rachelle Cracchiolo, M.S.Ed.

Science Contributor
Sally Ride Science

Science Consultants
Nancy McKeown,
Planetary Geologist
William B. Rice,
Engineering Geologist

Teacher Created Materials
5301 Oceanus Drive
Huntington Beach, CA 92649-1030
http://www.tcmpub.com

ISBN 978-0-7439-0564-0

Printed by: 51497
Printed in: China

Table of Contents

The Growing Universe

Did you know that the **universe** is getting bigger?

Thanks to astronomers such as Edwin Hubble, our view of the universe is getting bigger, too! His work, and a **telescope** that was named after him, have helped scientists learn about what exists beyond Earth.

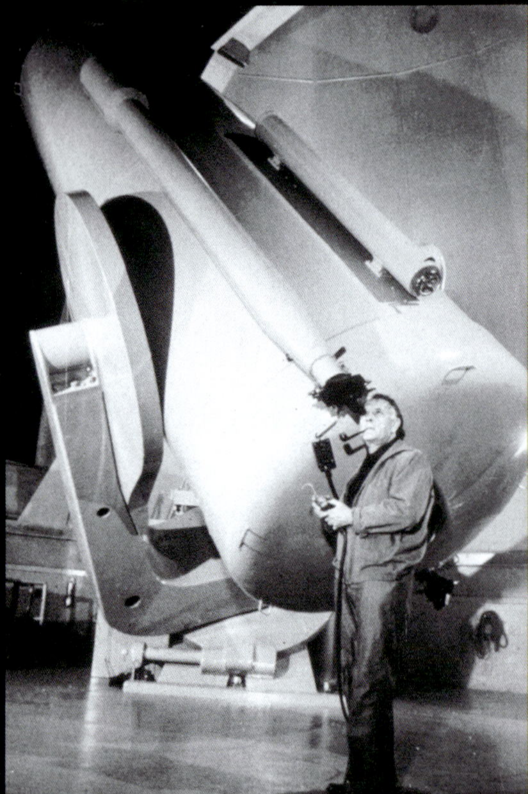

Until recently, people did not know much about outer space. We know Earth is the third-closest **planet** to our sun. We know that our planet is made of rock, is covered with water, and that life exists here. Other planets are harder to learn about.

Much of what we know comes from images taken by cameras on powerful telescopes. Telescopes allow us to see things far away—things we could never see without help. They allow us to look at other planets in our **solar system.** They have changed our view of the universe.

Beatrice Tinsley

(1941–1981)

Beatrice Tinsley led a short but important life. She studied galaxies and the age of stars. She won many awards for her work. After her death, a group of astronomers began a new award in her honor. It is given to a top researcher whose work is especially creative.

History of Astronomy

In ancient times, the planets and stars were a great mystery to people on Earth. Shepherds, sailors, and travelers were the first **astronomers**, or space scientists. They made many discoveries. However, some of their ideas were not correct.

Nicholas Copernicus

Copernicus' model of the solar system

Most people thought Earth was flat. They thought that Earth was the center of the universe. Some thought that the planets had magical powers.

The science of studying the **stars**, planets, and heavenly bodies is called **astronomy**. One of the first astronomers was Nicholas Copernicus. He was born in Poland in 1473. He argued that the planets in our solar system move around the sun.

Most people didn't believe Copernicus. But the books he wrote helped other astronomers figure out how the universe works. Copernicus died in 1543. He didn't know that one day he would be called the father of modern astronomy.

In 1491, Copernicus enrolled at the Cracow Academy in Poland, where he first learned about astronomy.

An Italian scientist named Galileo Galilei (1564–1642) built one of the first telescopes. A scientist from Denmark built the first one. Galileo heard about it and soon built a much better one. He used it to discover mountains and craters on the moon. He was able to watch stars and planets. He proved that Copernicus had been right. The planets did revolve around the sun.

People respect Galileo today. During his life, people did not want to hear his ideas. The church insisted that Earth was the center of the universe. The church put Galileo on trial in 1633. He was held under house arrest for the rest of his life.

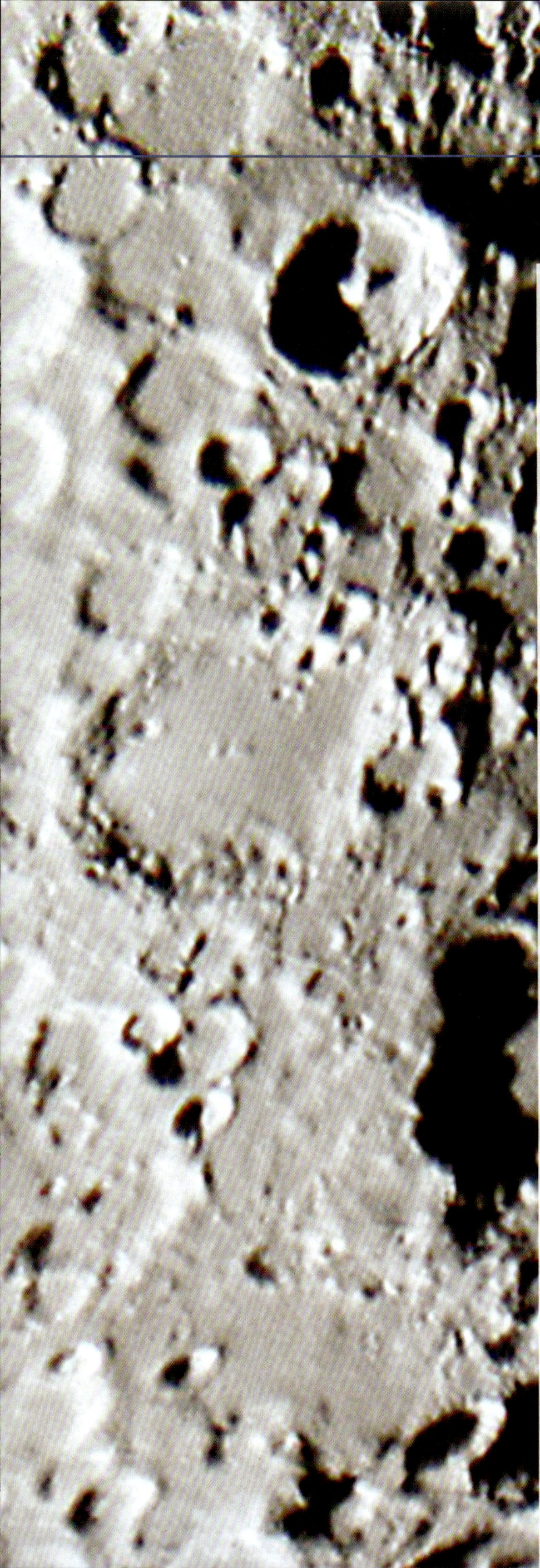

Johannes Kepler (1571–1630)

Johannes Kepler was a German astronomer and mathematician. He believed that Copernicus was right. Earth was not the center of the universe. Kepler studied how fast planets move and the shape of their **orbits**. These ideas are known as **Kepler's Laws.** Kepler is so important to the history of astronomy that craters on both the moon and Mars are named after him.

Over the next centuries, there were many people who studied space. However, the greatest advances in astronomy waited for more than two hundred years. For the most part, they came with the invention of new telescopes. The following pages tell of some important astronomers who used telescopes to do big things. Their work has taught all of us amazing things about outer space.

an astronomer operating a telescope in 1647

a telescope in outer space

an astronomer operating a telescope in 1933

Telescopes

Telescopes let us see faraway objects by making them bigger for the eye. They do that by collecting light from the distant object and bringing it to the eye. The lens or mirror in the telescope collects the light and brings it to a point of focus. A second lens spreads out the light.

You can make a very simple telescope with two magnifying glasses. You will also need a book. Open the book. Hold one magnifying glass above it. Hold the second glass between you and the first glass. Move the second glass up and down (like a trombone) until you can see the print of the book in clear focus. The print will be larger than it is without your "telescope." It will also be upside down.

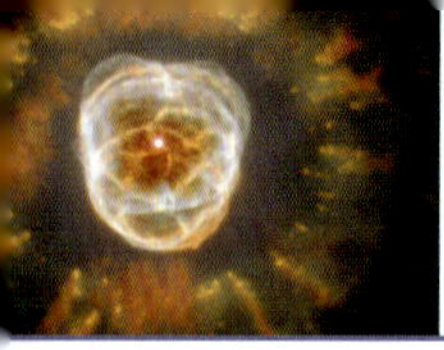

Edwin Hubble (1889–1953)

Edwin Hubble was one of the greatest astronomers of all time. He changed our view of the universe.

Hubble was born in 1889 in the United States. As a boy, he first learned to love science through the books he read. Books such as *From the Earth to the Moon* opened his eyes and mind to space.

Mt. Wilson Obervatory in California, where Hubble worked after the war

Hubble almost took a different career path. He first became a lawyer. He practiced law for a few years. Law did not make him happy, though. He knew he wanted to study astronomy. So, he went back to school.

His work in science was sidetracked once more due to World War I. He was a soldier in the war. When it was over, he was finally able to follow his heart. He took a job in an **observatory**. In this building, he was able to use a telescope to observe space.

Mary Fairfax Somerville
(1780–1872)

Mary Fairfax Somerville of England became a widow at a young age. Because she also had money, she was in a unique position. She was able to pursue her own interests. She loved science, and she began with the study of astronomy. Her studies led her to conduct her own research. In 1826, she became the first woman to present her own scientific research to the Royal Society of Astronomers in England. She published many science books in her life. The last one was at the age of 89!

Hubble found that there are other galaxies in the universe. He created a system to group these galaxies. He developed Hubble's Law in 1929. Using this law, scientists proved that the universe is still growing!

Hubble worked from a 100-inch telescope. This was the best telescope of his time. Today, astronomers use much more powerful telescopes. They also use telescopes in orbit above the earth. One of the best telescopes in space is named in honor of Hubble.

an astronomer operating a telescope in the early 1900s

the Harvard Observatory

Pickering's Girls

Annie Jump Cannon was born in 1863 in the United States. A childhood case of scarlet fever left her nearly deaf. That didn't stop her from doing what she wanted to do. In college, she studied **physics** and astronomy. Later, she went to work for Edward Pickering at the Harvard Observatory.

Pickering had a big job. He wanted to create a record of all the stars that had been seen in the sky. Cannon was one of the women astronomers who were hired to help. They were called "computers" because they used math to locate stars. These women became known as "Pickering's Girls." Together, the astronomers recorded over 400,000 stars. Cannon found a way to group stars that is still used today. Between 1911 and 1915, Cannon classified 5,000 stars per month!

Observatory Builder

George Ellery Hale was born in Chicago in 1868. He was the only child of wealthy parents. Hale made many contributions to astronomy. He even built an invention to study the surface of the sun. He did that while he was still in college!

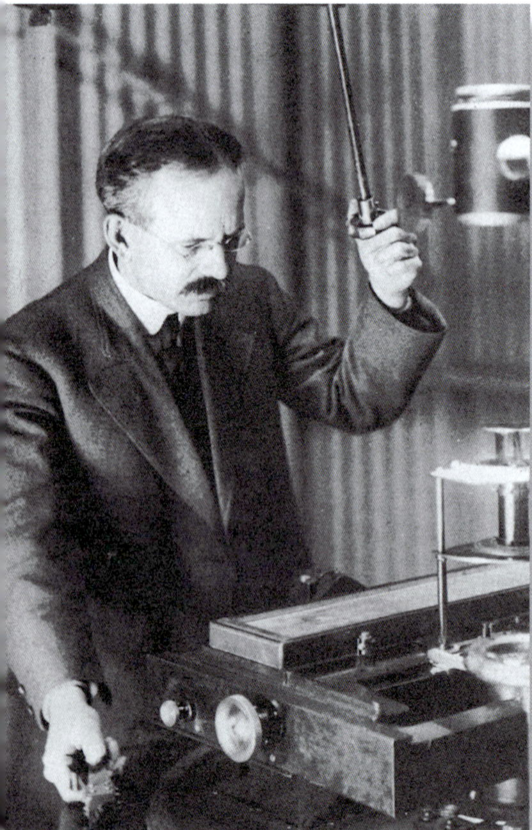

Amazingly, Hale became one of the most important astronomers of the 20th century with only a basic college degree. Most top scientists of the 20th century and beyond have higher degrees. They go to school for a very long time. Not Hale. Much of what he learned, he figured out on his own.

Hale loved astronomy. He spent most of his time thinking and studying and watching objects in space. He founded a new journal about astronomy. He even invented a new word in astronomy. It is **astrophysics**. That is the study of the physics and chemical makeup of bodies in space. He called his journal the *Astrophysical Journal.*

Hale's greatest achievement is not so much what he knew. It's what he did. Through hard work, persistence, and commitment, he made a big difference in astronomy. He was the founder of three great observatories.

Miss Mitchell's Comet

[1818—1889]

Maria Mitchell was born in 1818. She began watching stars at a young age. Her father had an observatory. Mitchell helped him with his work. In 1847, Mitchell discovered a new **comet**. The comet became known as Miss Mitchell's Comet. The discovery made her famous. In fact, Mitchell recorded many "firsts." She was the first person in America to sight a comet. She was the first woman to be named to the Academy of Arts and Sciences in 1848. She was also the first woman astronomy professor.

In 1895, Hale helped design the Yerkes Observatory in Wisconsin. In 1904, he founded the Mount Wilson Observatory near Los Angeles. He then helped build the first giant reflecting telescope. That is a telescope that uses mirrors. It measured 200 inches. It was installed at the Mount Palomar Observatory in California. It was the biggest telescope in the world for 30 years. It was named the Hale Telescope in his honor.

Hale's observatories led the field of astronomy for many years. Scientists used them to learn about galaxies and what they are made of. They used them to learn new things about the sun. Discovery after discovery was made in Hale's observatories.

Yerkes Observatory in Wisconsin was designed in part by Hale.

Mount Palomar Observatory in California

Carl Sagan (1934–1996)

Few people have made as big an impact on astronomy as Carl Sagan. He made astronomy popular with the general public. He wrote books about space and produced television shows about it. He worked on most of **NASA**'s unmanned space missions. When he died, the landing site of the *Mars Pathfinder* spacecraft was renamed the Carl Sagan Memorial Station in his honor.

Lyman Spitzer (1914– 1997)

Lyman Spitzer Jr. was one of the 20th century's great scientists. He was the first to propose placing telescopes in space.

Spitzer was born in Ohio in 1914. He studied physics and taught at Princeton for almost 50 years. He was known as a great teacher.

Spitzer was one of the world's leading experts on **interstellar matter.** That's the gas and dust between stars. He studied how stars and galaxies formed from this material. He also founded a lab that works on using **nuclear fusion** to produce energy here on Earth. Nuclear fusion is the source of the energy within stars.

a nursery of new stars

Lyman Spitzer

The Life of a Star

The Nobel Prize is given every year. In 1983, astronomer Subrahmanyan Chandrasekhar was awarded the prize in physics. Chandrasekhar was born in India in 1910. He found that when stars lose their energy, they collapse and become very dense. They become either white dwarf stars, neutron stars, or black holes. A **white dwarf** is a small, dense, hot star near the end of its life. A **neutron star** is a very small, superdense star made up of tightly packed neutrons. A **black hole** is an area in space where **gravity** is so strong that even light cannot escape from it.

The **Chandra X-ray Observatory** is named in Chandrasekhar's honor. It is a satellite observatory.

computer art of a black hole and material spiraling into it

Did You Know?

The Hubble Space Telescope was built to last for at least 15 years. Astronauts from the space shuttle make visits to Hubble so they can give it regular checkups.

In 1946, Spitzer suggested that an observatory in space would show much clearer images than telescopes on the ground. This was more than a decade before the first satellite was launched. In 1975, NASA began developing Spitzer's idea.

In 1990, 44 years after he first proposed it, Spitzer saw his dream become a reality. The Hubble Space Telescope was sent into space on a space shuttle.

The Hubble still orbits Earth today. It allows us to see objects clearly because it is above the clouds in Earth's **atmosphere**. The Hubble carries cameras that continue to send us amazing images of the universe. It runs on solar power. Scientists on Earth control it using radio signals. It is the first of the four Great Observatories NASA has sent into space.

Spitzer won many awards for his work in astronomy. He wrote many books as well. He was still working at Princeton when he died in 1997. He was 82.

In Honor of Spitzer

NASA named the last of its four Great Observatories after the scientist who first came up with the idea of putting telescopes in space. The Spitzer Space Telescope was launched in 2003. It uses **infrared light** to help astronomers see through clouds of dust in space. It has discovered new galaxies. It may also have recorded a faint image of the youngest star ever observed.

astronauts repairing the Hubble and adding new technology

Finding Pulsars

The thought that we might one day receive signals—or even a visit—from alien life has always been fascinating. In 1967, Jocelyn Bell Burnell thought she might have found just that.

Burnell was a university student in England. She worked with her advisor to help build a large telescope. Its goal was to pick up radio signals from space. Studying data from the telescope, Burnell found signals that could not be explained.

She and her teacher had no idea what the pulsing signals were. They named them LGM for Little Green Men. They thought they could be from aliens! Soon after, it was found that a spinning neutron star can make the pulsing signals. These objects became known as **pulsars**.

Burnell is now the head of the physics department at Open University in England. She has received many awards for her work. Her teacher received the Nobel Prize in 1974 for the discovery of pulsars.

Jocelyn Bell Burnell

The Crab Nebula is the remains of a star that exploded. The exploded star became a pulsar. It is at the center of the picture, surrounded by a blue glow.

Margaret Burbidge (1919–)

Margaret Burbidge is an important astronomer for many reasons. Her work added to our understanding of the rotations and masses of galaxies. She helped to figure out how elements are formed inside stars. She fought for career opportunities for other woman astronomers. Burbidge is especially important to the Hubble Space Telescope. She helped to design some of its original instruments.

Did You Know?

The radio telescope that Jocelyn Bell helped build was so big that 57 tennis courts could fit on land covered by it! She collected data in the form of lines on strips of paper. Burnell studied over 122 meters (400 feet) of chart paper from the telescope every four days.

Sally Ride Science

Geologist: Joy Crisp

NASA Jet Propulsion Laboratory

Rock and Rover

How do geologists study rocks millions of miles away on Mars? Joy Crisp did it with help from two busy little rovers. Scientists can't travel to Mars, so they send robotic rovers to be their eyes and ears.

Crisp led a team that decided what tools to give the rovers. The tools were used to analyze Mars' geology—its rocks and soil. The rovers made exciting discoveries. Some parts of Mars were once covered in water!

"We knew we wanted to look for things on rocks like ripple marks from water," Crisp says. Crisp's team chose cameras, drills, and other tools for the rovers. These tools identified minerals formed in water.

The rovers roamed Mars' rocky hills and rolled into its craters. They scraped rocks and snapped photographs. They beamed the data back to scientists on Earth. It proved that Mars, the red planet, was also once a wet planet.

Being There

If you were a geologist, you would study rocks and learn about the land and how it formed. As a geologist, you could also . . .

- investigate fossils hidden in rocks. Fossils help scientists understand the creatures that used to live on Earth.
- figure out where water, minerals, or diamonds are located.
- come up with solutions to environmental problems, such as soil and beach erosion.

How Do They Know?

Crisp and her team studied photographs of Mars rocks. The rocks look similar to ones on Earth that have been changed by water. Find a rock that's been shaped by water. How would you describe it?

About You

Crisp did not discover her love for geology until college. As a girl, she loved English, reading, and math. What are your favorite subjects?

Lab: Mini Constellation Viewer

Constellations are patterns formed by stars. Centuries ago, humans used their imaginations to link star patterns. They did this by drawing dot-to-dot pictures in their heads. They named the constellations after ancient gods, objects, and animals. After you do this activity, try to find some constellations in the night sky.

Materials

- 35mm film canisters (one for each constellation you want to view) or other such containers
- scissors
- tape
- pushpin
- constellation patterns (page 29)
- paper
- pen

Procedure

1 Choose a constellation from the patterns on page 29. Trace it and cut it out on the dotted lines. (If you have a copy machine, you can copy it that way.)

2 Tape the pattern in place over the bottom of the film canister.

3 Using a pushpin, punch a small hole through the paper and the canister for each star in the pattern.

4 Hold the film canister up to the light. You should see light through each hole.

5 Take the pattern off the canister. Trade with a partner and see if you can both figure out which constellation the other chose.

6 Try to find the same constellations in the night sky.

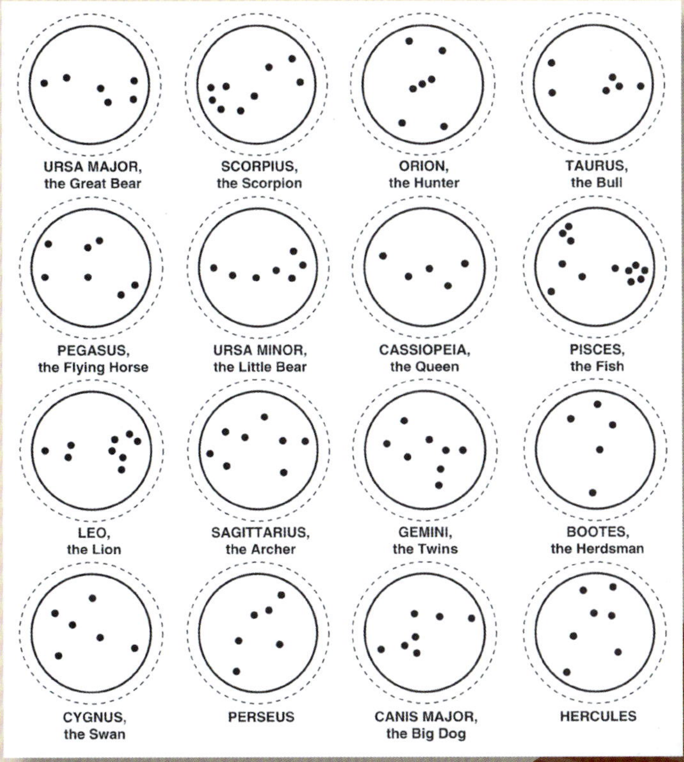

Glossary

astronomer—a person who studies celestial objects

astronomy—the study of the universe and of objects in space such as the moon, sun, planets, and stars

astrophysics—the study of the physics and chemistry of bodies in space

atmosphere—a layer of gases that surround a planet

black hole—invisible region in space with a strong gravitational field

Chandra X-ray Observatory—a NASA satellite that observes things in space, such as black holes and neutron stars

comet—icy and dusty object that orbits a star

gravity—the force of attraction between two objects

infrared light—electromagnetic radiation, with wavelengths longer than visible light but shorter than radio waves

interstellar matter—dust and other matter, including streams of protons, moving between the stars

Kepler's Laws—a series of three laws that explain planetary motion

NASA—U.S. National Aeronautics and Space Administration

neutron star—a very small, superdense star composed mostly of tightly packed neutrons

nuclear fusion—energy released in an atomic reaction in which two nuclei combine to make a larger one

observatory—places where you can use strong telescopes to view space

orbit—the path that a planet, moon, or celestial body follows around another body

physics—the science of matter and energy and of interactions between the two

planet—a celestial body that orbits a star and is the only object in its orbit

pulsar—spinning neutron stars that give off bursts of radio waves at regular intervals

radiation—emission of energy waves

solar system—the system of planets and other bodies orbiting the sun (other planets around other stars are called planetary systems)

star—a huge ball of gas that produces heat and light

telescope—an instrument made of lenses and mirrors that is used to view distant objects

universe—everything that exists anywhere

white dwarf—a small star that has run out of fuel

Index

Sally Ride Science

Sally Ride Science™ is an innovative content company dedicated to fueling young people's interests in science. Our publications and programs provide opportunities for students and teachers to explore the captivating world of science—from astrobiology to zoology. We bring science to life and show young people that science is creative, collaborative, fascinating, and fun.

Image Credits

Cover: NASA; p.3 NASA; p.4 (top) NASA; p.4 (right) The Print Collector/Alamy; p.4–5 Jurgen Ziewe/Shutterstock; p.5 Rick Reason; p.6 (top) Photos.com; p.6 (left) The Granger Collection, New York; p.6–7 The Print Collector/Alamy; p.7 Vieloryb/Shutterstock; p.8 (left) SuperStock, Inc./SuperStock; p.8 (right) The Granger Collection, New York; p.8–9 Thomas Nord/Shutterstock; p.9 The Granger Collection, New York; p.10 (bottom) SuperStock, Inc./SuperStock; p.10–11 NASA; p.11 Underwood Photo Archives/SuperStock; p.12 (top) NASA; p.12 (right) New York Times Co./Getty Images; p.12–13 Roger Ressmeyer/CORBIS; p.13 Library of Congress; p.14 Wellesley College Archives; p.14–15 CORBIS; p.14–15 (background) William Attard McCarthy/Shutterstock; p.15 Bettmann/CORBIS; p.16 (top) Jurgen Ziewe/Shutterstock; p.16 (bottom) The Print Collector/Alamy; p.17 F. Carter Smith/Sygma/CORBIS; p.17 (right) NOAA; p.18 Robert Goode/ Shutterstock; p.19 (top) Tony Korody/Sygma/CORBIS; p.19 James Steidl/Dreamstime.com; p.20 (top) NASA; p.20 (right) Time & Life Pictures/Getty Images; p.20 (bottom) NASA; p.21 (top) William Franklin Mcmahon/Time & Life Pictures/Getty Images); p.21 Chris Butler/Photo Researchers, Inc.; p.22 NASA; p.23 NASA; p.24 NASA; p.24–25 Robin Scagell/Photo Researchers, Inc.; p.25 NASA; p.25 (right) Hulton Archive/ Getty Images; p.26–27 NASA/Photo Researchers, Inc.; p.27 NASA; p.28 (top) Paul Maguire/Shutterstock; p.28–29 Nicoll Rager Fuller; p32 Getty Images